The Bandit

A Greek Myth Retold by Carolee Dean

HOT ROD Decodable Level 1

Littleton, Colorado

ISBN 979-8-9874895-7-4 (hardcover)
ISBN 979-8-9874895-6-7 (paperback)
ISBN 979-8-9874895-8-1 (ebook)
Library of Congress Control Number: 2023911731

First Edition Book, 2023

Book cover design, illustration, editing, and interior layout by:

www.1000storybooks.com

For G.G.

ACKNOWLEDGEMENTS

Thanks to my early readers, The Girls at the Abbey, and my consulting team: Paula Moraine, Mary Gilroy, and Lynn Kuhn.

Tiffany Strelitz Haber went through several drafts of the poetry section with me. She is the author of several rhyming picture books, and her expertise was essential.

Any inconsistencies regarding the above are mine alone.

NOTE

Pair and Share Reading is a strategy that pairs developing readers with proficient readers (educators, parents, or peers) who share the literacy experience by reading aloud the introduction at the beginning of the book. The developing reader then reads the poem, which was written to align with Level 1 of the HOT ROD Scope and Sequence. Level 1 targets closed syllables CVC, CCVC, CVCC, CCCVC...and words that incorporate the floss rule (ff,ll,ss). Multisyllabic words have been split into syllables for students who haven't yet learned syllable division.

The entire book may be read independently by students with fifth-grade or higher reading skills. Go to www.wordtravelpress.com for additional information and to find supplementary activities.

Watch for the chapter book version of the book, *Gods and Gifts*, coming soon!

Prerequisite Skills - Concepts that have previously been taught.

Targets: Single consonants including **s** as /s/ and /z/

  c = /k/ before a, o, u, & consonants, c = /k/ after a closed (short)

  vowel in two-syllable basewords

  Words containing the floss rule (final ff, ll, ss)

  Initial/final blends

  CVC closed syllables

Schwa - ə in the words: **a, the,** and in the second syllable of two-syllable words

Suffix **-s** as /s/ and /z/

Learned Words - These words need to be taught for two different reasons:

1. They contain irregular spellings and can't be decoded.

2. Although they are regular, their structure has not yet been introduced.

Irregular Words: do, of, to, was

Not yet introduced: for, then, when, with

Limited word list of open (long) vowels: he

Words with second syllable stress: a·**bet**, en·**trust**, fan·**tas**·tic, for·**bid**·den

Epimetheus (ĕp-ə-MĒ-thē-əs) - one of the Titans

Hephaestus (hə-FĔS-təs) - Greek god of fire and metalworking

Olympus (ō-LĬM-pəs) – home of the Greek gods

Olympians (ō-LĬM-pē-ənz) – the gods who lived on Olympus

Pandora (păn-DOR-ə) – the first human woman

Prometheus (prō-MĒ-thē-əs) – one of the Titans

Titans (TĪ-tənz) – the gods who came before Zeus

Vulcan (VŬL-kən) – the Roman name for Hephaestus

Zeus (zūs) – the king of the Greek gods

Olympians

Zeus

Olympus

Epimetheus

Titans

Vulcan

Prometheus

Zeus, the king of the Greek gods, asked two Titans to fill the world with living creatures. Epimetheus created the animals. He gave them all interesting gifts. Some received night vision. Others got tails they could use for swinging from branches.

Prometheus crafted a special creature out of mud. He called that creature "man." He wanted something that could think like the gods.

By the time Prometheus finished his special creation, his brother had given away all the gifts. Prometheus was upset that man didn't get anything special. In fact, man didn't get anything at all: not a feather, a fur coat, nor a prehensile tail.

6

Prometheus decided to go to Mount Olympus and steal fire. That would be his gift to the humans! He figured that if he took just a tiny flame, the gods wouldn't miss it. He hid it in a stalk of fennel. Then he ran back down to earth and gave fire to the people he had created.

With fire, people could stay warm and cook food. They could make swords, crowns, skillets, flutes, and toenail files. One day, mankind would even be able to melt cheese to make nachos!

Perhaps the most important result of this gift was that people were drawn together. They began to form a sense of community.

8

The Olympians were furious when they realized that Prometheus had stolen their fire. He had taken one of their most precious possessions and given it to mankind! Zeus was so angry that he chained the Titan to a cliff. Then he sent an eagle to torment him all day long.

Note: In some versions of the story, the eagle was a vulture. It's important to remember that Greek Myths are a lot like modern-day superhero movies. There are many versions of the same story.

The worst part of Prometheus's punishment was that he had to watch Zeus get his revenge on the humans. Mankind paid dearly for accepting the gift of fire, but that's another story about a woman named Pandora and a box.

Note: Vulcan is the Roman name for Hephaestus. He was the god of fire. The Romans "borrowed" the Greek myths, and then gave most of the Greek gods Roman names.

12

In a dim and dis·mal spot,

Vul·can kept an an·vil hot.

A ban·dit crept in with a plan
to get a help·ful gift for man.

He hid it in a fen·nel stem.
Will Vul·can pelt and pum·mel him?

16

The gal·lant ras·cal, fast and swift,
fled with the for·**bid**·den gift,
then sped with rap·id·ness and skill
to slip past sum·mit, bluff, and hill.

18

He crept in glens and can·yons, vast,
to get his gift to man at last,
then lit the twigs and trod·den logs
in dis·tant drifts and sod·den bogs.

20

When did the sul·len Vul·can spot
the glints of crim·son, red and hot?

"Grab the ras·cal! Get the plant!"
The fran·tic gods went on a rant.

"Trip him! Trap him! Nab him! Get him!
Stop him and do not a·**bet** him!"

He ran past pads and ponds in lands
with fun·nel webs and sil·ken strands.
He did not stop to sit and rest
but swept past cliff, and crag, and crest,
and left a hun·dred splen·did bits
in rus·tic camps with sand and pits.

24

Then men got spits and stuff to smelt;

lamps to craft, and wax to melt.

Bands met up with wist·ful grins

at dusk in bliss·ful, hid·den dens.

26

The grand·est gift he did en·**trust**

to com·mon men of mud and dust

was kin-dred bonds, as well as man's

pros·pects and fan·**tas**·tic plans.

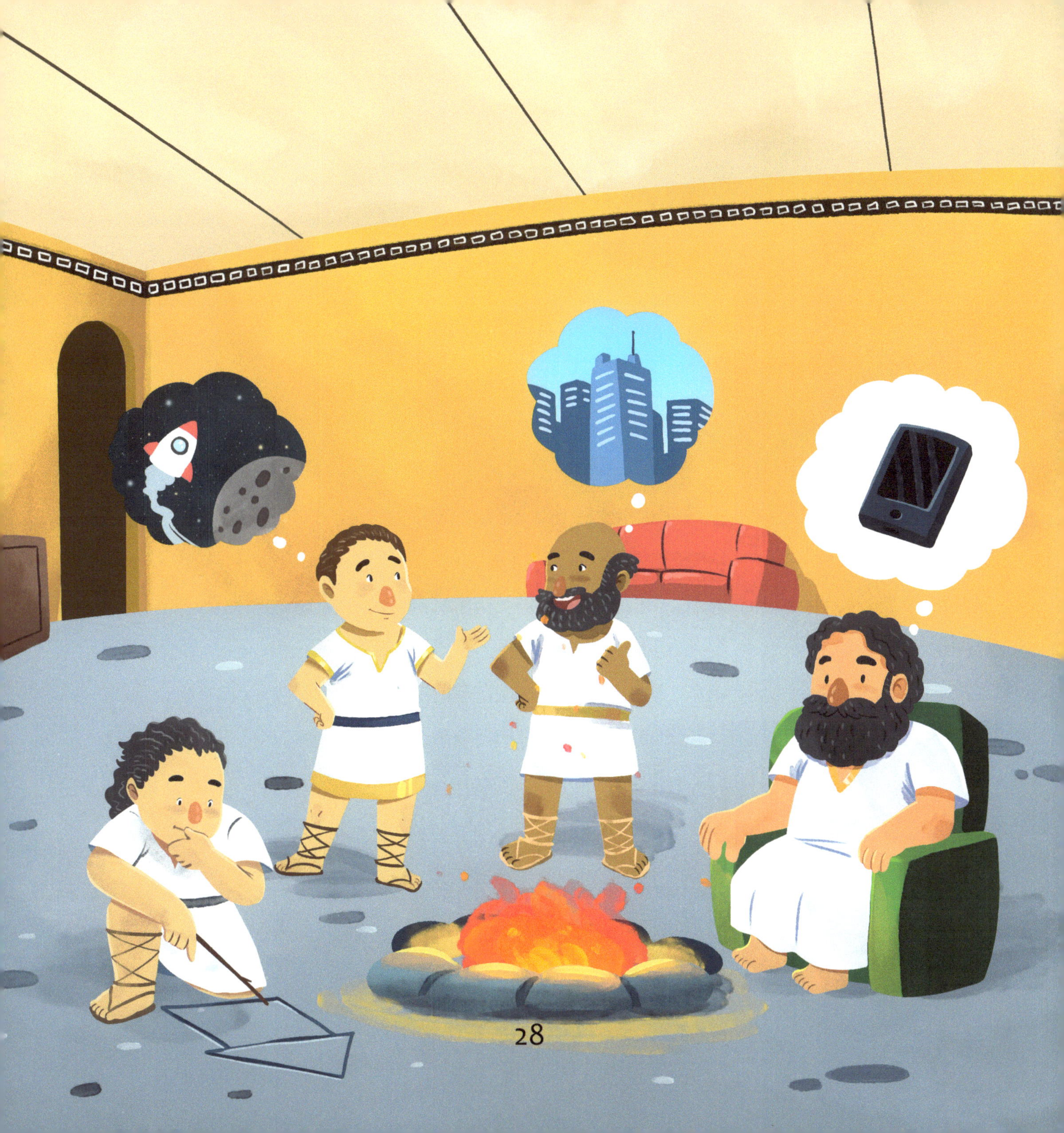

HOT Topics

1. Fire is useful for cooking food. What are some other ways that fire is useful to mankind?

2. A hot anvil and a hammer can be used to shape metal. Make a list of every-day things you use that are made out of metal.

3. Hephaestus was the Greek god of fire and metalworking. He made automatons out of metal. Automatons were metal statues of men that could move and help him in his workshop. They were a bit like modern-day robots. Have a discussion about the similarities and differences between the "men" that Hephaestus created and the men that Prometheus created.

4. If you had a robot, what jobs would you give it?

ABOUT THE AUTHOR

Carolee Dean, M.S., CCC-SLP, CALT is a speech-language pathologist and a Certified Academic Language Therapist specializing in the treatment of dyslexia. She is also the author of award-winning fiction for young adults and the educational resource: *Story Frames for Teaching Literacy: Enhancing Student Learning Through the Power of Storytelling* (Brookes Publishing, 2021). She combined her love of children's literature with her passion for helping struggling readers to create the HOT ROD series to promote Higher Order Thinking through the Reading Of Decodables.

www.ingramcontent.com/pod-product-compliance
Lightning Source LLC
Chambersburg PA
CBHW041604120626
46551CB00002B/304